W9-APO-865

McLEAN MERCER REGIONAL LIBRARY
BOX 505
RIVERDALE, ND 58565

A Message for my Child

Un Mensaje Para Mi Hijo

Written by
PATRICK ATKINSON

Illustrated by
ERNESTO ATKINSON

BEAVER'S POND PRESS

Textos en español en MensajeParaMiHijo.net

A MESSAGE FOR MY CHILD - ORIGINAL EDITION © copyright 1978, 2003, and 2011 by Patrick Atkinson. All rights reserved. No part of this book may be reproduced in any form whatsoever, by photography or xerography or by any other means, by broadcast or transmission, by translation into any kind of language, nor by recording electronically or otherwise, without permission in writing from the author, except by a reviewer, who may quote brief passages in critical articles or reviews.

ISBN 13: 978-1-59298-223-3

Library of Congress Catalog Number: 2011939113
Printed in the United States of America
First Printing: 2011
Second Printing: 2012
16 15 14 13 12   6 5 4 3 2

Cover and interior design by StudioCollective.com
Illustrations by Ernesto Atkinson

BEAVER'S POND
PRESS

Beaver's Pond Press, Inc.
7108 Ohms Lane
Edina, MN 55439-2129
(952) 829-8818
www.BeaversPondPress.com

To order, visit www.BeaversPondBooks.com or call 1-800-901-3480.
Reseller discounts available.

For all children young and old

SPECIAL THANKS

In the journey of life I've been one of the luckiest guys on earth, and have worked with some of the finest people imaginable. To them, and for all who read my works, I say thank you. In particular for this book, I'd like to thank Anthony Bramante of ITEMP for pulling this project together, Christopher Mathew of The GOD'S CHILD Project for his patience and support, Jon and Alyssa Thomas of Studio Collective for handling the lay-out concept and design, and Beaver's Pond Press, the publisher. My greatest thank you goes to my son, Ernesto Atkinson, for whom the message in this book was written when he was a teenager.

I can give you
life,
but I can't
live
it for you.

*Puedo darte una vida, pero no
puedo vivirla por ti.*

I can give you
instructions,
but I can't tell you
where to go.

※

*Puedo darte instrucciones, pero no puedo
conducirte a donde tu quieras ir.*

I can give you
liberty,
but I can't help you to
protect it.

○

Puedo darte libertad, pero no puedo contar con que la conserves.

I can teach you
the difference between
good and bad,
but I can't make the
decision
for you.

*Puedo enseñarte la diferencia entre el bien y el
mal, pero no puedo decidir por ti.*

I can give you
advice,

Puedo darte consejos, pero no puedo aceptarlos por ti.

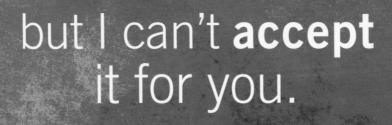

but I can't **accept**
it for you.

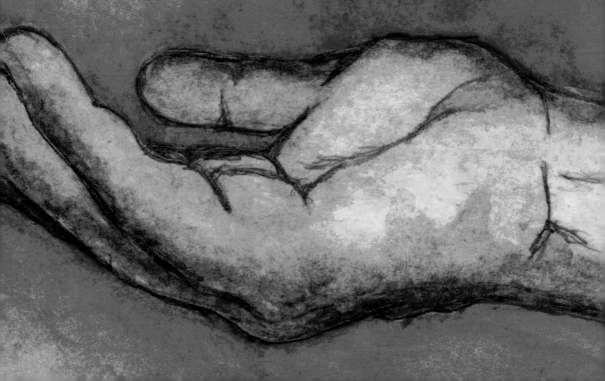

I can give you
love,
but I can't force you to
receive it.

*Puedo darte amor, pero no puedo
forzarte a recibirlo.*

I can teach you to
share,
but I can't stop
you from being
selfish.

Puedo enseñarte a compartir, pero no puedo evitar que seas egoísta.

I can teach you to

respect,

but I can't

make you be

respected.

✦

Puedo enseñarte a respetar,
pero no puedo forzarte a ser digno.

I can counsel you about your friends,

Puedo aconsejarte acerca de tus amigos,
pero no puedo escogerlos por ti.

but I can't **choose** them for you.

I can
teach you
everything you need to
know about sex,

•••

Puedo enseñarte todo lo que hay
que saber acerca del sexo,

but I can't
make you act
responsibly.

•••

pero no puedo hacerte actuar responsablemente.

I can
talk
to you about drinking,
but I can't say
"no" or **"just one"**
for you.

Puedo hablarte acerca de la bebida, pero no puedo decir "no" o "solo una" por ti.

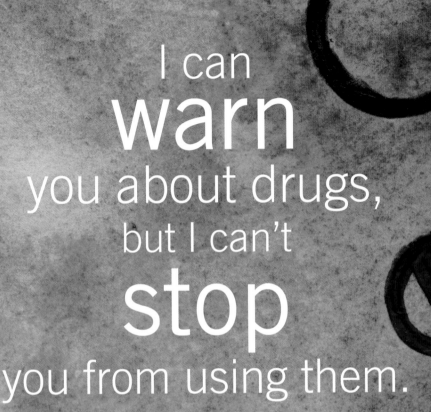

I can **warn** you about drugs, but I can't **stop** you from using them.

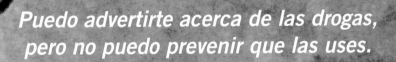

Puedo advertirte acerca de las drogas, pero no puedo prevenir que las uses.

I can talk to you
about having important

goals,

but I can't

achieve

them for you.

❧

Puedo hablarte de metas importantes,
pero no puedo alcanzarlas por ti.

I can teach you about **charity,** but I can't make you be **generous.**

*Puedo enseñarte lo que es la bondad,
pero no puedo forzarte a ser generoso.*

I can
pray
for you, but I can't
make you walk with
God.

♦

*Puedo rezar por ti, pero no puedo
hacer que camines con Dios.*

I can **talk** to you about how to live, but I can't give you eternal **life.**

♦

Puedo hablarte de cómo vivir, pero no puedo darte vida eterna.

When everything is **said** and **done**,

Al final de cuentas: cada uno decide por sí mismo y cómo va a llevar su vida.

everybody
decides for him or
herself how they will
live their
life.

I **love** you,
I **accept** you,

and I hope with all my

heart

that you make the right
decisions.

*Te quiero, te acepto y espero con todo mi
corazón que decidas lo mejor.*

ABOUT THE AUTHOR:
PATRICK ATKINSON

Patrick John Atkinson was raised in Bismarck, North Dakota and attended Minnesota State University– Moorhead. After graduation in 1981, Patrick turned down lucrative corporate job offers to work with runaways, prostitutes, and gang members in New York City's Hell's Kitchen. Two years later, Patrick moved to Central America where he began a twenty-five-year international career in war-zone reconciliation and post-war reconstruction. He has been knighted, is the recipient of numerous human rights awards (including the Guatemalan Congressional Medal) and is the subject of the biography, *The Dream Maker*, by Monica Hannan. Patrick is most proud of having been named Father of the Year by his son, Ernesto, this book's illustrator. He is the founder and executive director of The GOD'S CHILD Project and the Institute for Trafficked, Exploited & Missing Persons (ITEMP). When not being shot at, knifed, caught in car-bombings, or traveling worldwide advocating on behalf of abused, abandoned, or human-trafficking victims, Patrick resides in Central America and at Hippo Wallow Pond, his family home outside of Minneapolis, Minnesota.

PatrickAtkinson.com
The-Dream-Maker.com

ABOUT THE ILLUSTRATOR:
ERNESTO ATKINSON

Ernesto "Neto" Atkinson was born and raised in Antigua Guatemala. Even as a young boy, Ernesto expressed a great interest in art, and over the years his artistic influences grew with tremendous passion. After graduating from El Gran Moyas High School in 1999, Ernesto traveled the world where he explored the arts and understanding of the human existence. He attended North Dakota State University where he began an architectural career but later focused more on the arts. He graduated in 2007 with a degree in visual arts. He has been called "an artist who truly sees art as an active agent of change"; his work represents a contemporary movement which observes his experiences with everyday life, political and religious concepts, and philosophies. Ernesto's art is a mix of different media that represents the different faces and dissimilarities of society with her incomparable and multiple textures and colors. Ernesto resides in Fargo, North Dakota, works in education, and displays his art through galleries and online.

ErnestoAtkinson.com

ALL PROCEEDS FROM THE SALE OF THIS BOOK FEED, CLOTHE, AND HOUSE ORPHANED CHILDREN AT **GODSCHILD.ORG** AND **ITEMP.ORG**

CLEAN MERCER REGIONAL LIBRARY
BOX 505
RIVERDALE, ND 58565